essentials

essentials provide up-to-date knowledge in a concentrated form. The essence of what matters as "state of the art" in the current professional discussion or in practice. *essentials* inform quickly, uncomplicatedly and comprehensibly

- as an introduction to a current topic from your field of expertise
- as an introduction to a subject area that is still unknown to you
- as an insight, in order to be able to speak on the subject

The books in electronic and printed form present the expert knowledge of Springer specialist authors in a compact form. They are particularly suitable for use as eBooks on tablet PCs, eBook readers and smartphones. *essentials*: Knowledge modules from economics, social sciences and the humanities, from technology and the natural sciences, as well as from medicine, psychology and the health professions. From renowned authors of all Springer publishing brands.

Josef Gochermann

Technology Management

Recognizing, evaluating and successfully using technologies

 Springer

Josef Gochermann
Hochschule Osnabrück
Osnabrück, Germany

ISSN 2197-6708   ISSN 2197-6716   (electronic)
essentials
ISBN 978-3-658-36354-3   ISBN 978-3-658-36355-0   (eBook)
https://doi.org/10.1007/978-3-658-36355-0

Preface

Many of our current products and services would be inconceivable without the use of sophisticated technologies. The properties of products are based on technologies, such as in mechanical and plant engineering, automobiles, or smartphones, or the processes for manufacturing the products require technological solutions, such as in food industry or chemical industry. And many services cannot be provided at all without the use of computer and information technologies.

The selection of suitable technologies and their correct and beneficial use are therefore important components for market success. Making the required technologies available at the right time is one of the main concerns of technology management. In addition, it must be recognized in good time when the performance of a technology is exhausted and new technologies can pose a threat to it.

In the following sections, this compendium on the essential elements of technology management provides you with answers to ten essential questions on how to evaluate your technologies correctly, identify opportunities and risks in good time, and position yourself successfully in terms of technology. It is based on the contents of a basic lecture on technology management and allows a first introduction to the topic. It is aimed at anyone who wants to deal with the use and benefit of technologies, whether in development, product management, consulting, sales and marketing, strategy development, or corporate management. In addition, it can provide students of various disciplines with a basis for dealing with technologies.

Osnabrück, Germany

Josef Gochermann

Contents

List of Figures

List of Tables

Can Technologies Be "Managed"?

1

Technology does not mean hardware. In the original Greek sense, *technology* means "the process or art of producing objects commercially". Technology is therefore not hardware, but the knowledge of how to do something – the *know-how*. Engineering is the conversion of technologies into applicable hardware or software.

How and when technologies are developed, used or deployed can be assessed and planned. In most cases, the technologies used are the basis for an organization's range of services, i.e. for products or services. How good and how successful one is with it can be analyzed, evaluated, planned and executed and is thus subject to a structured management process.

Missed Technologies

What happens if you use your technological competence (the know-how = technology) in the wrong way or if you miss developments is shown by numerous examples even of renowned and so far successful companies.

For example, in the 1980s **IBM** completely misjudged the development of distributed computing technology as the basis of the personal computer (PC). IBM was the largest company in the US by revenue and the world leader in the computer hardware market. However, the computer market was manageable, there was a limited customer group that could afford the mainframes of the time, large corporations, government agencies, universities. At the beginning of the 90s, IBM wrote losses worth billions and had to lay off more than 200,000 employees.

© The Author(s), under exclusive license to Springer Fachmedien
Wiesbaden GmbH, part of Springer Nature 2022
J. Gochermann, *Technology Management*, essentials,
https://doi.org/10.1007/978-3-658-36355-0_1

Nokia, as well, has obviously missed a technology deployment. As the world's leading manufacturer of mobile phones, Nokia mastered and technologically led many of the technologies also used in today's smartphones years ago: Edit emails on the mobile phone, Internet access, calendar and data management, and many more. Only the technology use of the touch screen and the user-friendly tapping and swiping, the Finns have probably misjudged. Today, the former mobile phone division of Nokia belongs to the Microsoft group.

Many small and medium-sized enterprises (SMEs) have also failed to recognise technological developments or have missed technological opportunities. While corporations such as IBM and Nokia often have sufficient financial reserves to absorb such a setback, many SMEs have disappeared from the market as a result of a technology change.

Importance of Technology Management

A basic concern of technology management is to identify and implement far-reaching, risky technological product and process innovations in time and largely independently of the company's current level of success, so that a company's existence is never threatened as a result of missed technological innovation opportunities.[1]

Beyond this extreme case, technology management has far-reaching functions in the everyday innovation life of a company or organization:

Technology management has the task of making the *required technologies* available for *future services* at the *right time* and at *reasonable cost*. Thereby are

Required technologies	which provides the product or service with a benefit accepted by the customer
Correct time	at which the customer requests the product or service feature
Reasonable costs	equal or less effort to achieve the characteristics than the competitors

---

[1] Cf. Gerpott (2005, p. 6).

The selection of the required technologies presupposes knowledge of future developments. Technology management is therefore mostly future-oriented and always associated with significant risks that can rarely be captured in advance with classic planning tools.

How Do Technologies Change Over Time?

2

There are old technologies whose performance declines and newly developed technologies that replace others. The performance of a technology, its field of application and the benefits it generates change over time – technologies go through a **technology life cycle.**

Characterization of Technologies in Life Stages

The technology life cycle can be broken down into four phases: Introduction, Penetration, Maturity and Degeneration (see Fig. 2.1). In general, the diffusion of the technology, i.e. its beneficial use, is plotted over time.

The four technology states are characterized as follows:

Pioneering technologies	are only accessible with great effort, are often still in a state of development and can only be used by specialists; their distribution is still very limited.
Key technologies	are developed but not yet widely available and require good knowledge to tap into them; allow those who master and harness them to differentiate themselves from the competition.

© The Author(s), under exclusive license to Springer Fachmedien Wiesbaden GmbH, part of Springer Nature 2022
J. Gochermann, *Technology Management*, essentials,
https://doi.org/10.1007/978-3-658-36355-0_2

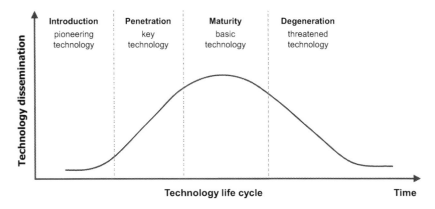

Fig. 2.1   The four phases in the technology life cycle

| **Basic technologies** | are established and form the basis for today's products and services; they are dominated by many and therefore offer little opportunity for differentiation. |
| **Threatened technologies** | are in the process of degeneration and are nearing the end of their useful life; are being substituted by other technologies. |

If one wants to differentiate oneself from the competitors through technology, one should

- choose a technology that is only mastered by a very few,
- be a leader or at least very good at mastering this technology, and
- combine as many technologies as possible to increase the complexity and to make copying more difficult.

The technology life cycle phases are often coupled with the life cycle phases of the products in which they are used. A product based on a pioneering technology is not yet widespread in the market. It is still at the beginning of the product life cycle with the new technology and the sales generated are low. Products with key technologies, on the other hand, are offered and demanded more and more, typical for the growth phase in the product life cycle. If the product has established itself in the market and is widely used, the technology is often also mature and is used by many. Market success no longer depends on the controllability of the technology, but much more on market positioning. A threatened technology also means danger for the products and services based on it. As soon as alternatives appear on the market, customers can switch abruptly (cf. Chap. 3).

What Is the Significance of the Technology S-Curve?

3

New technologies replace old ones (cf. examples IBM and Nokia in Chap. 1) and this often while the previous technologies are still successfully used in the market. The new technology "overtakes" the previous one. This overtaking process can be illustrated with the so-called **S-curve** (cf. Fig. 3.1).

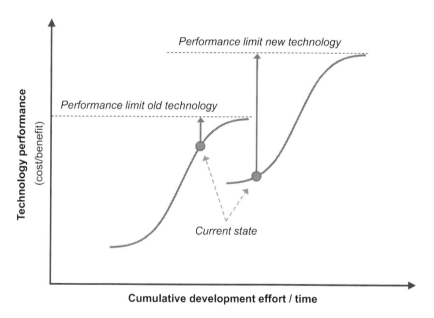

Fig. 3.1 Technology S-curve according to Krubrasik (1982), Foster (1986) (own illustration)

The S-curve concept is an empirical finding that was not developed from a theory. The S-shaped progression can be observed in a wide variety of technologies.

The X-axis shows the **cumulative development effort**, i.e. the added-up development effort; the more that is invested, the further you move to the right. Since this is a cumulative value, there is of course no movement to the left. The Y-axis illustrates the **performance of a technology** or the **benefit** that can be generated with it. This benefit can be of different kinds. For example, it can be measured by how much turnover is generated in the market with products and services based on this technology, or in how many different applications the technology is used. The benefits can also be very specific, such as how effectively the technology solves a specific problem. The achievable benefit of a technology usually correlates with the **technology attractiveness,** cf. Chap. 4.

The typical S-shaped course is as follows:

- The performance (benefit) and the application range of the previous technology are low at the beginning. A lot is invested in further development (X-axis to the right), but the performance increases only slightly (lower part of the S-curve).
- From a certain level of maturity, the performance increases rapidly without having to invest much in development (middle steep part of the S-curve). The technology has arrived on the market and is used in a wide variety of products and services – a high level of benefit is generated.
- At some point, however, the benefits and performance hardly increase any further, even if further investments are made in development (upper part of the S-curve). The technology then runs up against its **performance limit.**

Research and development are always working on new, better and more effective solutions. If a technology is successful in the market, new technological solutions are always being researched and driven forward. The goal is to achieve a higher benefit with an alternative solution. This technology will also go through an S-curve (right curve in Fig. 3.1):

- The newly invented or discovered technology then begins in principle at a higher performance level, even if this is still lower than for the current technology. It, as well, initially runs through the lower S-curve part and, despite noticeable development investments, its performance increases only slightly at the beginning.

- At some point, however, the new technology overtakes the old, achieves higher performance and offers greater benefits to the users. At this point, at the latest, users and customers will switch to the new technology.
- This technology will also run up against its performance limits at some time and is overtaken and replaced by a newer, more powerful technology.

Example: From the record to the CD to the digital down load
There are many examples of such technological changes. The S-curve development in the **recording and reproduction technologies for speech and music** can be recognized in a particularly impressive way. For many decades, the vinyl record was *the* essential medium through which music and speech could be stored and, above all, disseminated. The recording of speech and music on magnetic tapes and cassettes increased quality and flexibility, but was not able to displace the vinyl record. The record was steadily optimized, but ran up against a physical performance limit. At some point, the residual crackle and noise, due to the mechanical scanning of the grooves in the vinyl record, could no longer be reduced. The S-curve had reached the upper end.

The newly developed CD technology, on the other hand, started at a supposedly higher benefit level at that time. Digital recording was free of mechanical noise and, in addition, the performance and manageability of the CD was many times higher than that of the record. Within a few years the CD experienced an enormous boom. At the same time, the classic vinyl record almost completely disappeared from the market within a short time.

- In the meantime, however, the CD has also reached its performance limit, especially due to its size and limited storage capacity. The replacement by DVDs was followed by digital storage on other media. In the meantime, online streaming on the Internet is becoming more and more important. The storage medium is no longer in the foreground, storage is in the cloud.

The displacement of mobile phones by smartphones is another example of a rapid change in technology. NOKIA had missed this change and therefore almost lost its basis for existence (cf. Chap. 1).

However, both examples also show that a technology is rarely completely replaced. In other markets, with other target groups or in niche applications, displaced technologies can often survive for a long time. Millions of people in emerging and developing countries use classic mobile phones, as do many older people in industrialized nations. The record and its possibilities are still used by music professionals and DJ's and many a music lover still values the sound of a record more highly than the flat sound of a CD.

Identifying the right **time to change technology** is as important as it is difficult. Converting products and services to a new technology is costly and takes time. Products have to be revised or newly developed, production has to be converted and marketing has to be changed. On the other hand, offering two different technologies at the same time for a while is difficult to present in terms of production technology, logistics and market presence.

The timing of the switch is not easily to predict or determine according to rules. Both early and late switches have advantages and disadvantages:

- The early change to the emerging technology opens up the opportunity to be one of the first to offer the new solution to customers and thus to develop a stronger market position than subsequent providers. At the beginning, however, the risk is high, one does not know whether the new technology will prevail.
- On the other hand, the previous products and services are still successful in the market and generate profit. So you want to wait as long as possible before switching. However, if you switch too late, you run the risk of missing the connection and leaving the market to the other providers.
- Switching only when the new technology is already on par with the performance of the previous technology is not an option. It takes time to switch, know-how has to be built up, employees have to be trained. During this time, the use of the new technology is already well advanced.

Not only IBM or NOKIA have missed the technological connection. Many successful medium-sized companies, often successfully active in their industries for decades, also frequently miss the boat and suddenly disappear from the market within a few years.

This applies equally to product technologies as well as to production and process technologies. Both together are responsible for the ultimate product benefit and must be observed in a coordinated manner.

Prerequisites for determining the right time for a technology change are therefore

- knowledge of the current and future performance of the technology I use,
- the timely recognition of the emergence of new technologies, and
- the correct assessment of the market situation (customer acceptance).

To this end, it is necessary, on the one hand, to know the significance and current status of the technologies used (Chap. 4) and, on the other hand, to identify upcoming developments and new technological approaches to solutions at an early stage (Chap. 8).

Which Technologies Are Relevant for My Company?

4

Technology is an umbrella term. Technology is not just hardware, technology is know-how, the "knowing how" (cf. Chap. 1). This know-how relates to the most diverse fields of application and impact. Accordingly, technologies can be divided into different **types of technology**, depending on the area of application, type of use or share of the benefit (cf. Table 4.1).

For technology decisions in the company, it is important to know the technologies used and their importance for business success. In particular, it is important to master the **core technologies** that are indispensable prerequisites for the provision of services. These can be product-related as well as process technologies. However, other technologies are also responsible for the success of products and services.

The importance and influence of the technologies used can be determined with a **product-technology matrix** and brought into an easily assessable context. Each product or service is assigned which technologies are involved in its realisation and to what extent. The term product or service is understood to mean only that which generates a benefit for the customer.

The matrix rows are formed by the products and services offered by the company. The columns list the technologies used in the products, both those needed to realise the product functionalities or those needed for production or service provision (cf. Fig. 4.1).

© The Author(s), under exclusive license to Springer Fachmedien
Wiesbaden GmbH, part of Springer Nature 2022
J. Gochermann, *Technology Management*, essentials,
https://doi.org/10.1007/978-3-658-36355-0_4

Table 4.1 Overview of different types of technology (based on Zahn 1995, pp. 6–7)

Hard technologies (hardware-based: microelectronics, materials technology, biotechnology, laser technology …)	vs	**Soft technologies** (software technology, service technology, management technology)
Product technologies (are required for the realization of the product functions)	vs	**Process technologies** (required for the manufacture of the product, do not go directly into the product)
Core technologies (are a prerequisite for the realization and benefit of products and services)	vs	**Assistive technologies** (are necessary to make the products and services available)
Complementary technologies (cross-fertilize or complement each other in the development of solutions to problems)	vs	**Competing technologies** (arrive at comparable approaches to solutions on the basis of different knowledge)
Cross-sectional technologies (possess a wide range of application fields, e.g. electronics, optics)	vs	**Specific technologies** (have only relatively limited areas of application, e.g. petrochemicals, oil exploration)
System technologies (technology bundles for the manufacture of complex products, such as machines and apparatus, combination of different technology strands, e.g. precision optics/micromechanics/microelectronics)		

Product Technology Matrix for a company in the measurement and control industry ■ = core technology X = deployed technology O = weak influence		Electronics – EL	Components/control cabinet – CC	Digital control technology – DC	Modern bus technologies – MBT	Application programming – AP	Internet technologies – WWW	Database technologies – DB	Online remote maintenace – ORM	Optical fault detection – OF	Opt. process data acquisition – OP	
Plant control / hardware	PH	X	X	■	■							
Plant control / software	PS					■	X		X	O	O	
Electronic component design	ED	■	O									−
Machine data acquisition	MDE	O	O	X	X	■	X	■			O	+
Quality parameter detection	QP	O		X	X	■	X	X	X	■		+
Programming service	PR			X		■		O				
Optical recognition systems	OS	O	O	X	O		X	X		■	X	

Fig. 4.1 Product evaluation in the product technology matrix. (Cf. Gochermann 2004, p. 160)

A simple classification is sufficient for assessing the extent to which the technology is responsible for generating benefits:

Core technology	Indispensable prerequisite for the functionality and quality of the product or service.
Deployed technology	Technology to be used optimally for the realization of the functions or for the creation of the product or service.
Complementary technology	Is used to create the service, but could also be implemented differently.
Not used	Has no technological relevance to the product or service.

An example of such a product-technology matrix shows the analysis of a company for electronics development and measurement and control technology for industrial production plants.[1]

The company appears to be well positioned in the product groups "machine data acquisition" and "quality parameter acquisition" (cf. Fig. 4.1). Both product groups are based on two core technologies each and further technologies that are jointly responsible for the benefits. This **technological complexity** enables the company to differentiate itself well in the market (+). The danger that someone will be able to copy this technology combination is low. In the case of "electronic component development", on the other hand, there are hardly any possibilities for differentiation (−).

The matrix also allows conclusions to be drawn about the importance of the technologies used by the company (see Fig. 4.2). The two technologies "AP – application programming" and "www – internet technology" are important for the company as they are used in several products as core technology (+). The company must continue to be good at this in order to be able to hold its own in the market through technological competence.

The competences in the technology fields "KS – components/control cabinet" and "DB – database technologies", on the other hand, are hardly used for the realisation of the products (−). The cost of maintaining these competencies in the company cannot be justified by their use in the products. In this case, out-sourcing and purchasing as needed is recommended.

A product technology matrix

• identifies the relationships between technologies used and the products and services offered,
• highlights the products in which the supplier can hold its own by combining products
• shows which technologies to invest in for competence development and which to withdraw from.

The development of such a product technology matrix can be worked out in a workshop with the employees responsible for product management and technology development.

If one knows not only the importance of the technologies for one's own range of services but also the respective life phases of the technologies (see Chap. 2),

---

[1] Gochermann (2004, p. 160).

Product Technology Matrix — for a company in the measurement and control industry · ▨ = core technology · X = deployed technology · O = weak influence		Electronics – EL	Components/control cabinet – CC	Digital control technology – DC	Modern bus technologies – MBT	Application programming – AP	Internet technologies – www	Database technologies – DB	Online remote maintenace – ORM	Optical fault detection – OF	Opt. process data acquisition – OP
Plant control / hardware	PH	X	X	▨	▨						
Plant control / software	PS						▨	X	X	O	O
Electronic component design	ED	▨	O								
Machine data acquisition	MDE	O	O		X	X	▨	X		▨	O
Quality parameter detection	QP	O	O		X	X	▨	X	X	X	▨
Programming service	PR			X		▨	O				
Optical recognition systems	OS	O			X	O				▨	X
				–		+	+	–			

Fig. 4.2   Technology assessment in the product technology matrix. (Cf. Gochermann 2004, p. 160)

strategic decisions can be derived. If a technology is already a widely available basic technology and also has only a minor influence on my range of services – comparable to the technologies electronics and components control cabinet in the above example – then one should withdraw from this technology. If, however, a technology is still in an early phase and promises broad use in my products and services, there is a need for investment and development.

Is My Company Technologically Correctly Positioned?

A **portfolio** is a two-dimensional matrix for the graphical analysis and evaluation of business areas, products or technologies and for the derivation of standard strategies. One of the best-known portfolios is the BCG Boston Consulting Group matrix in which business areas and products are presented and classified in relation to their market position: Question Marks, Stars, Cash Cows, Poor Dogs. A good overview of different portfolio methods and their approaches can be found in Haag et al.[1]

Positioning in a portfolio is less concerned with the precise coordinate to be measured. Most portfolios divide into four quadrants to which standard strategies can be assigned. This makes it easy to identify whether one should selectively invest, hold or disinvest.

Not every two-dimensional matrix is a portfolio. In order to derive standard strategies, the two axes must differ from each other as follows:

Internal axis	Position can be influenced by own actions.
External axis	Position is determined externally and cannot be influenced or can only be influenced indirectly by one's own actions.

In the BCG market matrix[2] (see Fig. 5.1), the external axis is *market growth,* which a "normal" company can only influence to a very limited extent. The *relative market position* (internal axis), however, can be influenced by the company through market activities.

---

[1] Haag et al. (2011, S. 331).

[2] Boston Consulting Group portfolio analysis matrix.

J. Gochermann, *Technology Management*, essentials, https://doi.org/10.1007/978-3-658-36355-0_5

Fig. 5.1 Boston Consulting
Group matrix of market
positioning of products and
product groups. (Own
illustration)

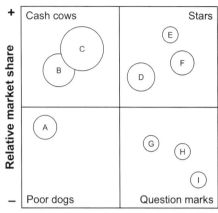

While the BCG matrix covers the market-product relations in a portfolio, the internal and external relevant criteria of a technology assessment are used as metrics in a **technology portfolio**.[3] Here, too, the axes must satisfy the distinction between external and internal:

Technology attractiveness	Sum of the economic and technical benefits that can be unlocked by the technology (external)
Resource strength/own technology position	Degree of own technical and economic mastery of this technology (internal)

Both are not necessarily numerically exact measurable variables, but describe the two criteria mostly qualitatively.

---

[3] The technology portfolio goes back to work by Pfeiffer et al. in 1982 and is still valid in its basic features today (cf. also Pfeiffer et al. 1991).

Technology attractiveness is an external variable and can only be influenced by the company to a limited extent. Whether a technology is attractive is influenced by external factors. Possible evaluation variables can be:

Further development potential	To what extent is further technical development possible in the area in question? How great is the potential for qualitative improvement?
Application range	In how many different areas of application can a benefit be generated with the technology? How should the spread of the technology be assessed in terms of the number and scope of areas of application?
Effort and risk	How high is the time and financial effort to further develop the technology and how high is the risk of not finding an adequate solution to the problem?
Dissemination speed	How quickly will the technology spread in the market? Are there acceptance barriers in society or with customers to overcome and how high are these?
Synergetic benefit	How high can positive synergy effects on other technologies or products of the company be?

How well I master the technology and what the company's **own technology position** is the internal variable that depends on the company's decisions and activities. It is also often evaluated in relation to the competitor and then called **relative technology position**. Possible evaluation criteria are[4]:

Development resources	How are the financial, human and material resources required for further development to be assessed in comparison with the competition?
Know-how	How well is my technology protected against competitors by patents and other intellectual property rights or by trade secrets?
Level of control	How well do I master the technology used and how well can I integrate it into marketable products and services?
Realisation speed	How quickly can the technology be integrated into marketable products and services, and how quickly can technical advancements be realized compared to the competition?
Complementary technologies	Are the complementary and application technologies required for successful implementation available at upstream and downstream stages of the value chain? How well does the corresponding information exchange function within the company (knowledge management)?
Strategy support	How strongly does the technology support the strategic goals and competitive strategy of the company or business unit?

---

[4]Cf. Seibert (1998, p. 154).

The axis dimensions are difficult to evaluate in exact numerical values – and this is not even necessary. Often one divides the axes into three fields "low – medium – high". The classification in the portfolio position can be made by assessment of experts in the company on the basis of facts available or to be researched. Ultimately, it is about the assignment to certain fields in order to make a decision for the selection and expansion of a technology and not primarily about the exact position in the diagram. Possible standard strategies[5] are shown in Fig. 5.2.

The example in Fig. 5.3 shows the distribution of the technologies used by a technology-based medium-sized company. Regardless of the position of the individual technologies, the distribution alone allows a general assessment. The company is poorly positioned technologically. The company has a good command of those technologies (high relative technology position) that have a low attractiveness, while it has a weak own position in the attractive technologies. In a good distribution, the technologies would be distributed along a diagonal from bottom left to top right.

Fig. 5.2 Standardisation strategies in a technology portfolio. (Own illustration)

	low	medium	high
high	**Select** rationalise		**Invest** technology leadership
medium			
low	**Disinvest** retreat		**Select** improve

Relative technology position

Technology attractiveness

[5] Adapted from Pfeiffer (1991).

Fig. 5.3 Technology
portfolio of a medium-sized
technology company. (Cf.
Gochermann 2004, p. 161)

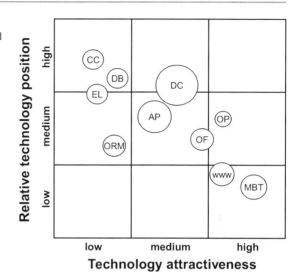

The company would therefore have to try to better master the interesting
technologies (MBT, WWW, OP), keep the quite attractive technologies (AP,
DC), withdraw from the unattractive technologies (e.g. outsourcing) and per-
haps observe not so interesting technologies (e.g. ORM) with regard to their
future attractiveness.

How Can I Improve My Technology Position?

6

Positioning technologies and competencies in technology portfolios (Chap. 5) allows the derivation of standard strategies depending on the position in the portfolio (cf. Fig. 5.2). Basically, there are two dimensions in which one can improve one's position:

- **Increasing the level of mastery of the technology**

and

- **Increasing the attractiveness of the technology or switching to a more attractive technology**

Increasing the **degree of mastery** means increasing the ability to optimally realise the benefits of technology and thereby differentiate from the competition. The following measures are suitable for this:

- Qualification of relevant employees (design, development, technical sales, etc.)
- Hiring new employees with current expertise, such as college graduates who bring fresh knowledge to the table.
- Poaching qualified employees from the competitor
- Cooperation projects with knowledge providers (universities, research facilities) to generate fresh knowledge
- Participation in technology and innovation networks
- Investment in modern development and laboratory equipment

- Acquisition of companies with the required expertise
- Structuring of technology and innovation management in the company
- and much more.

Increasing the **attractiveness** of the technology used so far is only feasible to a limited extent for an individual company and usually involves a great deal of effort. In the case of a **technology pioneer** who has developed and applied this technology for the first time, the attractiveness can be increased through improved exploitation of the potential benefits, for example through

- improvement of performance parameters, e.g. accuracy, speed, quality,
- further development of the functionalities,
- facilitation of usability (integration into the environment, operability, etc.),
- adaptation to further areas of use and applications,
- reduction of technology-specific costs,
- stronger protection through patents.

The **switch to a more attractive technology** should be carefully considered. The S-curve described in Chap. 3 is helpful here. In order to make a switch decision, the following questions should be answered:

- Has the potential of my technology really been exhausted or can I generate further benefits with reasonable effort?
- In which life cycle phase is the new technology and how quickly and with what effort can its benefits be increased?
- Do I have the necessary know-how to use the new technology in-house?
- How high are the switching costs (investment, personnel, knowledge) and how do they relate to future market returns?
- Is there a need to switch to follow an industry trend? Will we be left behind otherwise?

Ultimately, the question of how to **procure the new technology** remains to be clarified. Basically, there are three possible ways to make[1] the new technology usable for my company:

- Use of internal technology sources
  - Own research and development (R&D)
  - Advantages: technological independence and exclusivity
- Cooperative technology procurement
  - Contract research (e.g. to institutes)
  - Collaborative research, cooperation projects
  - Technology and innovation networks and alliances
  - Joint ventures and shareholdings
- Acquisition of rights and know-how from external technology sources
  - Acquisition of licenses from know-how owners
  - Technology acquisition

In Germany, as in most industrialised countries, numerous R&D institutes are available as development partners. These institutes and facilities cover a broad research and development spectrum, both in terms of technical-scientific disciplines and in terms of the level of knowledge and market proximity. The appropriate partner must be selected depending on the life phase of the technology (cf. Chap. 2; Fig. 2.1) and on the scientific and technical state of knowledge:

- Basic research (knowledge-oriented)
  - University research, Max Planck Institutes, Helmholtz research centres, German Research Foundation, etc.
- Applied research (application-oriented)
  - Universities of applied sciences, Fraunhofer Society, Leibniz Society, independent institutes of applied research, etc.
- Industrial research (sector-oriented)
  - Development departments of industrial companies, industrial research centres and institutes, chamber of trade training centres, AiF Arbeitsgemeinschaft industrieller Forschungsgemeinschaften (German Federation of Industrial Research Associations), etc.

---

[1] Cf. Schulte-Gehrmann et al. p. 73.

The technology S-curve (see Chap. 3) illustrates that other technologies with a higher benefit for the customer can compete with established technologies. In the worst case, they replace them. In the literature, competing technologies are therefore also referred to as **substitute technologies**.

> **Competing technologies** solve a problem in a different functional way than before. The **benefit** for the user is higher than with the previously used technology (less effort, more output).

Competing technologies must therefore always be evaluated from the **user's or customer's point of view**. Following the marketing principle that "people don't buy things, people buy problem solutions", it is not the technology itself that is the decision argument, but the way in which the problem can be solved with less effort or with greater benefit.

The original version of this chapter was revised. The correction to this chapter can be found at https://doi.org/10.1007/978-3-658-36355-0_11

© The Author(s), under exclusive license to Springer Fachmedien Wiesbaden GmbH, part of Springer Nature 2022, corrected publication 2022
J. Gochermann, *Technology Management*, essentials,
https://doi.org/10.1007/978-3-658-36355-0_7

Example: Drilling Machine and Bonding Technology

Drills are bought to drill holes with. For example, in the wall to insert a dowel, to screw in a hook and thus hang up a picture. The customer does not buy drilling machines because he wants to drill, his benefit is to fix the picture to the wall. A competing technology to the drilling technology in this case is the gluing technology. It allows the attachment of objects without destructive drilling and dirt. Therefore, leading manufacturers of adhesives already advertise with the slogan "gluing instead of drilling".

Technologies become dangerous to my technology when they perform the desired function in other technological-knowledge-based ways. To identify such competing technologies, one must describe and compare technologies in terms of their functions. **Function analysis** is used to identify the relevant features. It provides a systematic representation, classification and evaluation of the functions as well as their relationships according to the principle of effect (DIN EN 1325, VDI 2803):

- Capture of all information and data that reflect the characteristics of a technology.
- No assumptions or hopes, just name objective and feasible functions.
- Naming of functions is done by simple **noun-verb combinations**: e.g., welding = *metals * bonding* or *bonding * metals*.

Subsequently, one can look for principles that also fulfil the function "bonding metals *", for example riveting or gluing. Such technologies are often found in completely different fields of application and markets.

But how do one find these other solutions for the same function? And which ones are comparable at all? The **technology tree** represents a systematic approach. Starting from basic scientific principles or basic technological approaches, all possible solutions are systematically listed and broken down further and further into technical realization. In the lowest level of this quasi upside-down tree, all theoretically possible technical solutions to the problem are listed next to each other.

Figure 7.1 shows such a technology tree for a specific problem. The underlying problem arises from a very concrete technical application. In our everyday life, we find numerous rotating products and elements in which energy must be transmitted in the rotating state, mostly electricity. Examples are revolving entrance doors of buildings, production robots, turntable ladders on fire engines, cable drums on loading cranes, moving surgical lights in operating theatres and many more. Often

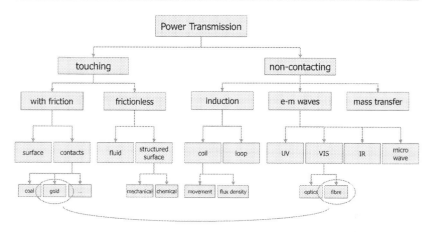

Fig. 7.1 Technology tree for the "Energy transmission" use case. For reasons of overview, not all possible variants have been entered. (Own illustration)

cables cannot be used because they would twist and tear during rotation. The technological issue therefore relates to the **transmission of energy in rotating systems**. Conventionally, contacting methods are often used, such as carbon or gold brushes on slip rings. Which technologies could pose a threat to this contacting technology? There are also non-contact power transmission technologies, but can these also be used in existing applications?

The question of energy transmission is first divided into the two possibilities "touching" and "non-contacting". The touching transmission can happen "with friction" or "frictionless", via surfaces or contacts, or by means of liquids or microstructured, frictionless surfaces. The technical implementation then results in the lowest row, for example by means of touching gold contacts.

In the case of non-contact approaches, three basic ways are initially conceivable: by induction, by means of electromagnetic waves or (hypothetically) by mass transfer ($E = mc^2$). Induction could be realized by coils or by a conductor loop; in the case of a coil, motion or flux density change would come into question. In the case of electromagnetic waves, the whole spectrum from ultra-short wavelength to extremely long wavelength can be imaged, here ultraviolet radiation, visual, infrared and microwaves as examples. The transmission of visual light could be done, for example, by imaging optics or by optical fibres.

At the lowest level, the technologies are now comparable. It is possible to evaluate whether in a specific application the technology "light transmission by optical fiber" can replace the transmission with "touching gold contacts" used so far. This depends, among other things, on the amount of energy to be transmitted (current intensity), the design conditions and boundary conditions, the influence of environmental factors and others. It is important to break down the solution approaches to as concrete a level as possible in order to be able to decide whether this technology can perform the described function "energy*transmission" in the required specifications.

How Do I Identify New Technologies at an Early Stage?

8

The early identification of emerging technologies is called **technology forecasting**. The aim is to pick up and interpret technology-relevant (weak) signals in the corporate environment at an early stage in order to be able to access information more quickly than competitors when making decisions about the company's technological innovation activities. The aim is to become aware faster than the competitor of

- further development potential of new technologies,
- limits of known technologies,
- substitution relationship between technologies, and
- expected breaks in the development of technologies (= technological discontinuities).[1]

In addition to the identification of competing technologies (danger), the focus is also on the recognition of potentials (opportunities). There are two basic approaches for technology forecasting. The non-directed, technology- and business field-independent investigation is referred to as

- **Technology Scanning**
  - Similar to a radar, one scans the technological developments in different fields and markets.

---

[1] Cf. Gerpott (2005, p. 101 ff.).

- Serves to identify technology-related opportunities and risks beyond the current technology portfolio.
- Is done undirected and independent of a business segment.
- Organisationally, it is usually a staff function at the overall company level.

If one wants to specifically predict the development of the technologies used in the company so far, one makes use of

- **Technology Monitoring**
  - The obvious competing technologies are continuously monitored and evaluated with regard to their potential threat.
  - Serves the targeted collection and interpretation of external events and developments for used technologies.
  - Definition of technology fields relevant to monitoring required.
  - Concerns mostly the core technological competencies.
  - Organisationally, it is usually decentralized in the business units.

Both orientations are based on intensive research work. In addition to the intensive analysis of secondary sources, such as patent and literature analyses, there are also a number of primary sources from which information can be obtained, for example customers, suppliers and research institutes.

Especially in the globalized environment, it will only be possible to a limited extent to notice and follow all technological developments. Often, however, it is sufficient to identify important trends and to recognize which principles of action emerge again and again. The following channels can be used to obtain and evaluate data on current developments without too much effort:

Scientific and technical conferences   Analysis of the conference programs. If the speaker is a professor from an (academic) university, then the technology is usually a bit further away from the market than if the speaker is the development manager of a technology company.

Trade journals (technology *and* market)   Regular reading of technological journals by developers and product managers provides current trends and is part of everyday work. The money for such subscriptions is well invested.

Newsletters and blogs from research institutions   Newsletters from R&D institutions, especially applied R&D, are not annoying email spam, but valuable sources of information about the state of the art. Blogs also contain references to topics that are still under consideration.

Innovative customers Among a company's customers are often also very innovative and forward-looking ones. They are concerned with the development of technologies and markets and with future developments. In a workshop, you can harness this knowledge for yourself. These customers like to get involved because they benefit from your company becoming better.

Innovative suppliers Suppliers supply many companies and therefore know the changing requirements. In addition, they have to constantly develop their own service portfolio in order to be competitive. They are often well informed about technology trends within the industry but also across markets.

Visiting trade fairs Trade fairs do not primarily serve to promote sales, but are *the* industry marketplace for the latest information, including on current technological developments. Since all relevant market participants are represented, it is easy to make a comparative assessment.

Open innovation is the opening up of the innovation process of companies and the strategic use of the outside world to increase their own innovation potential. Customers, suppliers and other partners can provide valuable information on new technological developments. Targeted surveys or half-day innovation workshops tap into this information.

Internal sources of information There is more information in your own company than you might suspect. The sales department knows the technological trends among customers and competitors, the marketing department has information about future customer needs and the development department is up to date on technical innovations. The systematic collection of this information creates an initial basis for future technology assessments.

Knowledge and innovation networks In many industries, knowledge and innovation networks consisting of companies, knowledge institutions and associations have been established. The goals are often the generation of new knowledge for the sector and the initiation of innovations. Get involved in these networks.

Regardless of which sources and channels are used to gather information, it is important that the information is gathered and evaluated **systematically and continuously**. Expert knowledge only in the heads of individuals does not help. For this purpose, it is necessary to clearly define the respective **search fields at** the beginning. The information needs are on three different levels[2]:

Quality level (how?) Requirement for the quality of the information: Timing (How early?) – Information content (How accurate?) – Validity (How certain?) – Exclusivity (How exclusive?).

Purpose level (why?) What the information is needed for: Determining technological potential, market potential, transferability to another technology field, disposition of production resources, or conformity with socio-political developments?

Object level (where & what for?) The content dimension of the information to be obtained and the definition of the search fields: Competencies and technical capabilities, functionalities of existing applications, capital and fixed assets, trends.

Search fields can be delimited with the help of portfolio analysis (cf. Chap. 5) or with technology trees (cf. Chap. 7).

---

[2] Cf. Wellensiek et al. (2011, p. 99).

Can Technology Forecasts Be Trusted? 9

Technology management often deals with future developments, new technologies and their use in future products and services. In addition to the analysis of the current situation, special importance is therefore attached to methods and instruments that provide reliable and resilient forecasts of future developments. Two methods of forecasting the future have emerged as particularly practicable and manageable.

The **Delphie method** is a structured, convergent expert survey. It was originally developed for long-term technological forecasts. Experts are interviewed several times in successive rounds until the statements converge. The experts can thus react to the assessment of their colleagues.

The name Delphi technique goes back to the oracle in the temple of Apollo in Delphi. According to legend, the high priestess Pytha sat there above a crevice in the earth, from which intoxicating vapors rose that put her into a kind of trance. Her prophecies were so vague that those seeking advice did not get a satisfactory answer the first time. They went home, thought about the answer, and then went to the oracle again. This was repeated. Gradually the answer – or rather the interpretation of the answers given by the oracle – became more concrete and sharper.

Of course, the Delphi method is carried out today without the use of intoxicating fumes. The decisive characteristic, however, is the back-and-forth between question and answer. However, the respondents are not an oracle but a group of experts or scientists. The Delphi methodology is based on the assumption that experts in their field can make particularly well-founded forecasts about future developments.

J. Gochermann, *Technology Management*, essentials, https://doi.org/10.1007/978-3-658-36355-0_9

As a rule, 20 to 50 experts, who are not allowed to coordinate among themselves, form a Delphi panel.

The experts are given a previously clearly defined forecast problem, for example *"What will be the degree of development of hydrogen technology in the motor vehicle sector in 10 years?"*, to which they must respond in writing. In addition to a question, the experts can also be presented with theses which they must comment on. These answers and comments are then evaluated with regard to their direction and consistency and combined into one or more trend answers. This assessment is fed back to the experts with a request to comment, clarify or expand on it. The returned answers are again clustered, combined into trend answers and again fed back to the experts. This process continues – usually about three times – until the answers converge. The result is a fairly reliable expert-based assessment of the state of the future. Sometimes two divergent convergences emerge, but even then two relatively clear possible future states can be identified.

The procedure of a Delphi forecast usually follows the following scheme:

1. Selection of a forecasting problem
2. Selection of experts to deal with the problem
3. Written questioning of the participants
4. Collection and evaluation of responses
5. Return of the results to the experts with the request to comment on the individual answers in comparison to the group results
6. Communication of comments to all experts
7. Re-interrogation round according to point 3–7 to
8. Convergence ⇒ Stop!

The advantages of the Delphi method are:

- Universally applicable
- Large time horizon: Suitable for forecasting technology fields and technological developments
- Location-independent and flexible in terms of time
- Prompt exchange of information via the Internet
- Well combinable with other methods (scenario technique, roadmaping …)
- Manageable effort.

The Delphi methodology, often also referred to as Delphi study, can be used very well for clearly delimited questions in technology development. It is usually organised and conducted by a Delphi team.

The **scenario technique is** suitable for more complex questions about the future. However, it can sometimes be very complex, which makes it not an everyday tool. Nevertheless, it is an excellent planning and control instrument for future developments. The typical time horizon for scenario building is 10–15 years.

Many people associate the term "scenario" only with the extremes "best-case scenario" and "worst-case scenario". However, these only form the outer boundaries of the scenario funnel (see Fig. 9.1). However, it is much more decisive to find out which possible future states in between will occur with what probability in the observation horizon.

The special feature of the scenario technique is that it does not simply develop different images of the future. These images of the future are constructed from consistent causal relationships. In the end, one knows not only the probable future state, but also *the path to it.* This opens up the possibility of checking over time

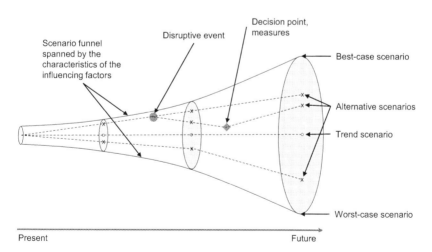

Fig. 9.1 Scenario funnel. (Adapted from Geschka & Hammer, 2005, p. 468; Nee, 2017)

whether one is on the predicted path or whether there are deviations. Have marginal parameters changed? Have events occurred that were not expected (disruptive events, see Fig. 9.1)? Since one knows the predicted path and can perceive deviations, corrections and changes are possible.

In order to construct this "plannable" future, the scenario technique goes into great detail. The scenarios are systematically developed from the current situation. To do this, one first identifies all possible factors that influence the picture of the future. These influencing factors usually come from five different areas: macroeconomical, technological-scientific, ecological-natural, social and political-legal (cf. Figure 9.2).

The best way to determine the influencing factors is to hold a workshop in which participants from different specialist areas or company divisions take part. The goal is to generate as complete a list as possible of all influencing factors. However, it is important not to overlook any of the essential factors. Depending on the breadth of the question, between 40 and 150 influencing factors can be gathered. However, these factors have varying degrees of influence on the development, some are negligible, others clearly shape the development.

Fig. 9.2 Areas of influence on the key factors of scenario building. (Own illustration)

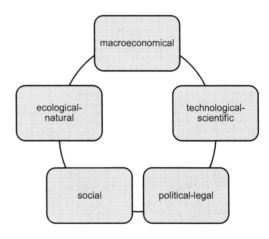

The next step in the scenario technique is to identify the essential factors, the **key factors**. As a rule, one finds between 10 and 20 factors that strongly influence the future picture. The next step is to try to predict the future development of these key factors. What technological developments will there be? How will society change? What possible paths might legislation take? What will happen if there is a change of government? And so on. This prediction can involve a considerable amount of research, which makes the scenario technique so costly. As a rule, one finds two to five possible development paths for each key factor, to which probabilities are assigned in the following. With 10–20 key factors and two to five possible development paths, there are several hundred possible scenarios – even if some combinations can be excluded for reasons of plausibility. Clearly, the most likely scenario results from the developments of the key factors with the highest probabilities, the least likely case from those with the lowest. However, developing the other realistic scenarios is quite complex. However, very powerful software is now available for setting up the necessary consistency matrix and for calculating the scenarios.

But let's get back to the core of the scenario technique. It is not about describing the most probable future state with the highest possible accuracy. Since one has derived the possible developments for the most important influencing factors, the key factors, on the basis of research and developed the scenarios from this, one can now check very precisely whether the path will be followed further, what reasons there are for deviations and how one can react to them.

How Do I Strategically Plan the Use of New Technologies?

When which technology is needed for which purpose and when it should be used is determined by the **technology strategy**. It is part of the innovation strategy, which in turn is part of the corporate strategy. Without clearly formulated corporate and innovation goals, it is not possible to develop a resilient technology strategy (see also Fig. 10.1).

Technology selection Determines which current and future technologies are addressed in the technology strategy. This applies technologies that are already in use as well as technologies that are not yet in use but exist, but also completely new technologies to be developed.

Technological performance How close to the state of the art do I want to operate? Do I want to be a **technology leader** or do I prefer to operate at a normal performance level. Attention: **State of the art** does not mean "what is common", but describes "what has just become technically possible through research and development", i.e. the front line of technological development.

Technology sources Where do I get the technology and the associated know-how? Do I carry out my own development and do I have the resources for it? Or do I procure the technology externally? Possibilities for this are development contracts with research and development institutions, cooperation projects with companies and institutes, but also the purchase of technologies or the acquisition of licenses (see also Chap. 6).

J. Gochermann, *Technology Management*, essentials,
https://doi.org/10.1007/978-3-658-36355-0_10

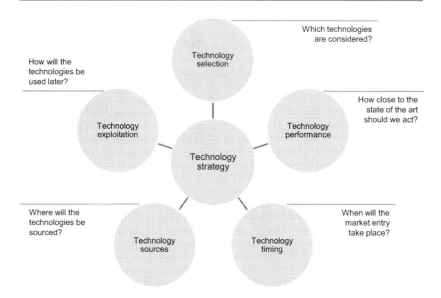

Fig. 10.1 The different dimensions of a technology strategy. (Based on Schulte-Gehrmann et al. in Schuh & Klappert, 2011, p. 67/68)

Technology timing   The timing of the deployment of new technologies describes both the development phase (invention timing) and the time of market entry (innovation timing). **Technology pioneers** are the first to develop new technologies and also introduce them to the market as technology leaders. **Technology followers** use the pioneer technology at a later point in time and try to make the best possible use of previous experience with the technology.

Technology exploitation   The technologies used in my products and services create benefits for the user. Can I also use the technological knowledge and the acquired know-how to generate further revenue? Into which other services of my company can the technology be integrated? Can I develop broader potentials together with strategic partners or in networks? Or can licenses be granted for the use of my technology?

In order to be able to correctly assess the need for development, the current state of development must be known with sufficient precision. A scale that has become widespread in the R&D world is the so-called **TRL – Technology Readiness Levels**. This was originally developed by the US space agency NASA to evaluate its space technologies and to estimate the time to market. The TRLs describe the respective **maturity level** of a technology under development. They have now become the standard for evaluating other future technologies as well. The European Commission, for example, has defined them as a classification of the development status of technologies in funding programmes (cf. Table 10.1):

These classifications are practical and separate the individual development stages well from one another. It is indeed a difference whether the technology has only been tested in the laboratory (TRL 3), works under relevant application conditions (TRL 4) or already performs as desired in the actual application field (TRL 5).

In order to plan future developments and to determine when which technology should be available in which form, various methods can be used. The **scenario technique** describes future states and the path to them on the basis of key factors. In a **Delphi study**, experts are questioned several times in successive rounds until congruent opinions emerge (cf. also Chap. 9). Once the picture of the future has been found, it is possible to determine backwards when which technologies will be needed and how long the development periods for them may be. This is usually done with the aid of a **technology roadmap**.

A technology roadmap is an analogy to a road map. It serves to visualize objects and paths, dependencies and causalities, objects that lie on the way, and provides

Table 10.1   Technology Readiness Levels (TRL) of the European Commission

TRL 1	Basic principles known
TRL 2	Technology concept formulated
TRL 3	Experimental proof of concept
TRL 4	Technology validated in the laboratory
TRL 5	Technology validated in the relevant environment (industrially relevant environment for key technologies)
TRL 6	Technology demonstrated in the relevant environment (industrially relevant environment for key technologies)
TRL 7	System prototype demonstration in operational environment
TRL 8	System complete and qualified
TRL 9	Actual system proven in operational environment (competitive manufacturing for key technologies)

European Commission (2017), Annex G

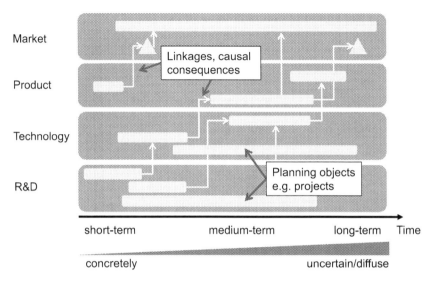

Market

Product

Technology

R&D

Linkages, causal consequences

Planning objects e.g. projects

short-term   medium-term   long-term   Time

concretely   uncertain/diffuse

Fig. 10.2 Basic structure of an integrated technology roadmap with four planning levels. (Own illustration, adapted from EIMRA, 1997; Schuh et al., 2011; Nee, 2017)

measures of the effort and time required to achieve certain goals. The roadmap supports the manager at the wheel in steering his entrepreneurial vehicle purposefully through unknown terrain.[1]

Technology roadmapping has established itself as a standard planning and visualization method in large parts of industry. The European Industrial Research Management Association (EIMRA) has proposed a basic structure for a road (see Fig. 10.2), which underlies most of the numerous roadmapping variants.[2]

A technology roadmap is always developed and built backwards. With the help of market research or the use of forecasting techniques (cf. Chap. 9), future market and customer perspectives are first identified and it is determined when the company wants to be in the market with a certain service. The market developments, including expected changes in legislation or changes in customer requirements, are shown in the chronological sequence in the top block "Market". This determines when the company must or wants to be ready with the development of the corresponding services ("Product" block). In the "Technology" block, it is now

---

[1] Möhrle and Isenmann (2017); Schuh et al. (2011).
[2] EIMRA (1997).

determined backwards when which technology development must be initiated and completed and when other required technologies must be available in order to be on the market with the products and services in time. If new knowledge, new materials or new processes are required, activities in the "R&D – Research and Development" block will also be necessary.

From the planning with a technology roadmap, it can then also be seen when which activities need to be parallelized and how much effort will be required. This is the basis not only for the necessary project planning, but also for resource planning.

Correction to: How Can I Recognize Competing Technologies and Alternative Solutions?

Correction to:

Chapter 7 in: J. Gochermann, *Technology Management*, essentials,
https://doi.org/10.1007/978-3-658-36355-0_7

The original version of the chapter was inadvertently published with an error in the title. It has been corrected as given below:

How Can I Recognize Competing Technologies and Alternative Solutions?

The updated original version for this chapter can be found at
https://doi.org/10.1007/978-3-658-36355-0_7

What You Can Gain from This Essential

- The importance of the relevant technologies in the company can be assessed.
- The technology benefit is measurable and influenceable.
- Technologies have different importance in the respective life cycle phases.
- Competing technologies can be identified and evaluated at an early stage.
- Technologies can be used strategically in the company.
- Technology management is important for successful innovation and product management.

References

The contents described and the figure shown are based on the author's lecture "Technology Management" at the Osnabrück University of Applied Sciences. The lecture is based on diverse and constantly evolving literature bases as well as on the findings from the author's own research projects, company projects and investigations.

Basic Elements of Technology Management Are Described in the Following Books

Albers, S., & Grassmann, O. (2005). *Handbuch Technologie- und Innovationsmanagement*. Gabler.

Amelingmeyer, J., & Harland, P. E. (Hrsg.). (2005). *Technologie und Marketing*. Wiesbaden: Gabler.

Gerpott, T. J. (2005). *Strategisches Technologie- und Innovationsmanagement* (2. Aufl.). Schäffer-Poeschel.

Gochermann, J. (2004). *Kundenorientierte Produktentwicklung – Marketingwissen für Ingenieure und Entwickler*. Wiley VCH.

Laube, T., & Abele, T. (2006). *Technologie-Roadmap*. Fraunhofer IRB.

Schuh, G., & Klappert, S. (2011). *Technologiemanagement, Handbuch Produktion und Management 2*. Springer.

Spath, D., Linder, C., & Seidensticker, S. (2011). *Technologiemanagement – Grundlagen, Konzepte, Methoden*. Fraunhofer.

Wördenweber, B., & Wickord, W. (2008). *Technologie- und Innovationsmanagement im Unternehmen* (3. Aufl.). Springer.

Zahn, E. (1995). *Handbuch Technologiemanagement*. Schäffer-Poeschel.

© The Author(s), under exclusive license to Springer Fachmedien Wiesbaden GmbH, part of Springer Nature 2022
J. Gochermann, *Technology Management*, essentials,
https://doi.org/10.1007/978-3-658-36355-0

Publications Cited in Addition

European Commission. (2017). *Horizon 2020, Work Programme 2016–2017, Annex G.* https://ec.europa.eu/research/participants/data/ref/h2020/other/wp/2016-2017/annexes/ h2020-wp1617-annex-ga_en.pdf. Accessed 15 Sept 2019.

European Industrial Research Management Association (EIMRA). (1997). *Technology roadmapping; Delivering business vision* (Working group 52 report). European Industrial Research Management Association (EIMRA).

Foster, R. N. (1986). *Innovation. Die technologische Offensive.* Gabler.

Geschka, H., & Hammer, R. (2005). Die Szenario-Technik in der strategischen Unternehmensplanung. In D. Hahn & B. Taylor (Eds.), *Strategische Unternehmungsplanung – Strategische Unternehmungsführung. Stand und Entwicklungstendenzen* (S. 464–489). Springer.

Haag, C., Schuh, G., & Kreysa, J. (2011). Technologiebewertung. In G. Schuh & S. Klappert (Hrsg.), *Technologiemanagement, Handbuch Produktion und Management 2* (S. 309 ff.). Berlin: Springer.

Krubrasik, E. (1982). Technologie: Strategische Waffe. *Wirtschaftswoche, 36*(25), 28–33.

Möhrle, M. G., & Isenmann, R. (2017). Grundlagen des Technologie-Roadmappings. In M. G. Möhrle & R. Isenmann (Hrsg.), Technologie-Roadmapping, Zukunftsstrategien für Technologieunternehmen (4. Aufl., S. 1–15). Berlin: Springer.

Nee, I. (2017). *Technologieplanung, im Rahmen der Vorlesung Technologiemanagement, Hochschule Osnabrück.* Campus.

Pfeiffer, W., Metze, G., Schneider, W., & Amler, R. (1991). *Technologie-Portfolio zum Management strategischer Zukunftsgeschäftsfelder* (6. Aufl.). Vandenhoeck & Ruprecht. (1. Aufl. 1982).

Schuh, G., Klappert, S., & Orilski, S. (2011). Technologieplanung. In G. Schuh & S. Klappert (Hrsg.), *Technologiemanagement, Handbuch Produktion und Management 2* (S. 55 ff.). Berlin: Springer.

Schulte-Gehrmann, A.- L., Klappert, S., Schuh, G., & Hoppe, M. (2011). Technologiestrategie. In G. Schuh & S. Klappert (Hrsg.), *Technologiemanagement, Handbuch Produktion und Management 2* (S. 55 ff.). Berlin: Springer.

Seibert, S. (1998). *Technisches Management.* Teubner.

Wellensiek, M., Schuh, G., Hacker, P. A., & Saxler, J. (2011). Technologiefrüherkennung. In G. Schuh & S. Klappert (Hrsg.), Technologiemanagement, Handbuch Produktion und Management 2 (S. 89 ff.). Berlin: Springer.

Printed in the United States
by Baker & Taylor Publisher Services